hand-made habitats

GARDEN

Paul Wright

Photographs by Robert Pickett

A & C Black · London

First published 1992
A & C Black (Publishers) Limited
35 Bedford Row, London WC1R 4JH

ISBN 0-7136-3549-5

A CIP catalogue record for this book
is available from the British Library.

Acknowledgements

Illustrations by Patricia Newell of John Martin and
Artists Limited.

Photographs by Robert Pickett, except for: p4b K. A.
Wilson, Papillio; p10b Michael Maconachie, Papillio; p13t
K. A. Wilson, Papillio; p15b Philip Marazzi, Papillio;
pp16/17 Chris Beddall, Papillio; p17b Philip Marazzi,
Papillio; p30t, m Eric Gilbert, Papillio.

The author and publisher would like to thank the staff and
pupils of Bolshaw Primary School, Bredbury Green Junior
School, Lum Head Primary School and Eardley Junior
School whose help and co-operation made this book possible.

Filmset by Rowland Phototypesetting Limited,
Bury St Edmunds, Suffolk
Printed in Italy by Imago

Contents

° DIARY °

SPRING

Hazel
Catkins

SUMMER

Buttercup

Ladybird

AUTUMN

Garden habitats

For thousands of years, people have made gardens so that they can enjoy the beautiful colours, shapes and scents of flowers. As their gardens grew, people discovered that plants attract many kinds of birds, bees, butterflies and other creatures.

Flowers don't just grow in man-made gardens. An amazing variety of wildflowers grow in meadows. A meadow is not planned and planted with flowers, but grows up naturally over hundreds of years. Each meadow has its own special mix of plants, and the birds and insects that live with them.

Meadows do need some human attention. Without regular mowing, a meadow would soon turn into dense undergrowth, in which flowers would struggle to survive.

◀ **A Comma Butterfly on a Buddleia bush.**

Each year, the grass in a meadow is cut to make hay for farm animals. All the food, minerals and nutrients which have been produced by the grass as it grows are taken away. This makes the soil very poor. Meadow flowers have had to adapt to live in places where few other plants can grow.

When the meadow is cut each year, all the flowers are cut with it. But the seeds of some flowers drop onto the ground and survive there through the winter, ready to spring up again the following year. Over the years the meadow develops its own mix of flowers. Some meadows are hundreds, even thousands of years old.

This book will show you how to make your own garden or wildflower meadow on a patch of ground at home or at school. You don't need much space and the plants you grow will provide food and shelter for many birds, insects and mammals.

◀ **Wild Buttercups growing in a meadow.**

Planning a small-scale garden

A garden can be any size. Any patch of ground will do, even if it's covered in concrete. Wildflowers can be grown just about anywhere.

Begin by finding a place at home or at school where you can make your garden. Decide whether you want to have a theme for the garden.

You could choose to plant a scent or a colour garden, or even a herb garden. Think about growing everlasting flowers such as Strawflowers or Acrocliniums for decoration, or plants such as Stinging Nettles which can be used for dyeing.

Herbs

Basil

Chives

Mint

Parsley

Sage

Thyme

Scented Plants

Honeysuckle

Ramsons
(Wild Garlic)

Evening
Primrose

Night
Stock

Rose

Plants for a blue/purple colour garden

Cornflower

Forget-
me-not

Bluebell

Foxglove

Thistle

Buddleia

You could even grow plants such as Dandelions and Horseradish for eating. (Make sure that you find out which plants are safe to eat before you taste <u>anything</u> in your garden.) With careful planning, you could mix many of these plants in a small area.

Use reference guides to help you to choose the plants for your garden. There is a list of useful reference guides on page 32. A visit to a local park could give you some good ideas, too.

What will you use to grow your plants in? You could use old tyres filled with soil or make a raised flower bed out of bricks. Most plants don't mind what they grow in. If there are paving slabs in your garden area, perhaps you could lift one of them and plant into the soil underneath?

Traveller's Joy   Honeysuckle

Ivy

Cotoneaster

Buddleia

Lawn planted with Red and White Clover, Camomile and wild grass seeds.

Don't just think about the ground level of your garden. Plants can be grown in hanging baskets, along fences and over walls, and even up strings and wires. Think about including window boxes, or using a trellis for climbing plants to grow up.

Make a scale plan of the garden showing which plants you have decided to include.

7

Planning a larger-scale garden

You may be lucky enough to have a larger area of ground at home or perhaps a playing field at school in which to make your garden. You could think about designing a meadow or a larger, more formal garden.

Could you find room for both a cultivated garden and a meadow area? These two environments complement each other very well.

Here are some things to think about when you're deciding what sort of garden to plant on a large area of land.

● Can you build the garden near a window? This will make it easier to observe the garden and the creatures which visit it.

◀ **A wildflower meadow.**

● What will you use to make the garden paths? Flagstones make good paths, but they are heavy and can be expensive. Gravel and bark chippings are cheaper than flagstones and they provide good habitats for minibeasts. Mowing a strip across the grass is the quickest and easiest way of making a path, but the grass needs to be cut at least every two weeks between April and October.

● If possible, plan some kind of seating in the garden – a bench, or perhaps a tree stump.

● Flower gardens need regular hoeing and weeding. Who will be responsible for this? You will need several friends to help you to keep the garden looking good.

● Meadows need much less maintenance. Once established, they just need to be cut and raked over at the same time each year.

● Is vandalism likely to be a problem? Meadow areas are almost impossible to vandalise, whereas flower gardens can be damaged more easily.

Attracting wildlife

Think about the different creatures you would like your garden or meadow to attract. You could plan to include a butterfly corner, a bee border or a bird patch.

Some flowers depend on insects to carry pollen from one flower to another to help them to reproduce. These flowers usually have bright colours and sweet smells to attract insects.

Hold a piece of black paper under a flower and gently brush the inside parts of the flower with a paintbrush. Transfer the pollen you collect on to the black paper.

If possible, examine the grains of pollen under a microscope. Can you discover why pollen is so good at sticking to creatures such as bees?

Some flowers, such as Foxgloves, are designed especially for bees to land on. Foxgloves have dots inside each petal which guide the bee to the inside of the flower where it can collect nectar and pollen.

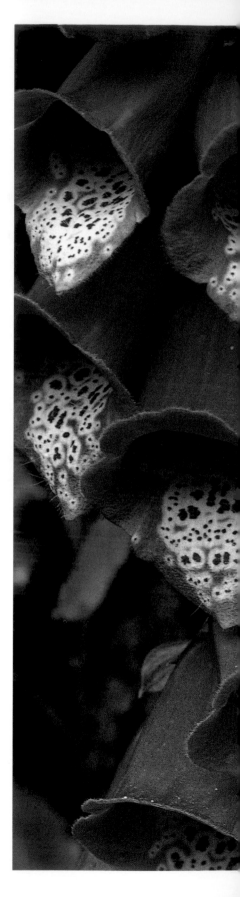

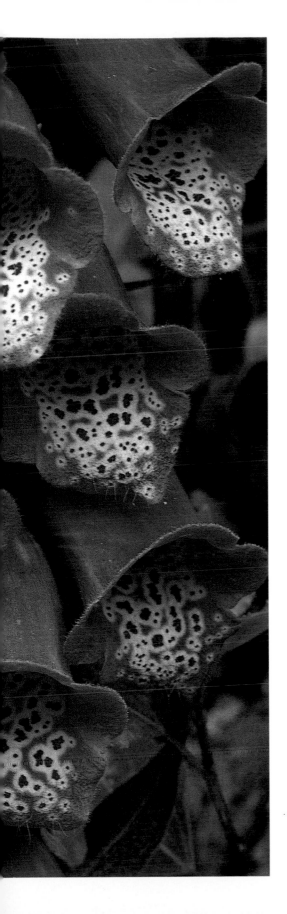

Stinging Nettles, Thistles and other common wild plants are very important food plants for caterpillars. If you don't want to include these plants in your flower garden, you could plant them in a wild patch somewhere close by.

If you plant a hedge around all or part of your garden, it will provide a home for many insects and birds. You will also be making a protected habitat for some of the hedgerow and woodland plants which people have removed from the countryside to make way for farmland.

Plants such as Oak, Holly, Yew, Laurel, Ash, Elm, Hawthorn, Guelder Rose and Willow all make good hedges.

Try to include a wall somewhere in your garden, the older and more crumbly the better. Butterflies will enjoy sunning themselves on it. Spiders, snails and even lizards often shelter in the cracks in walls.

A pond or marshy patch will attract a wide range of insects and birds as well as frogs and other amphibians. Ponds can be any size – an old margarine tub makes an ideal mini-pond. If you'd like to build a pond in your garden or wild area, use a reference book to help you.

You can encourage frogs to inhabit your garden by providing a variety of habitats including a ditch, long grass, stones, pieces of clay pipe and old, broken flower pots for them to shelter in.

Small mammals such as mice, voles and hedgehogs can also be attracted into your garden. You can make a hedgehog heap or a mammal mound quite easily. All you need to do is to pile up some dead tree branches and cover the heap with grass cuttings or rotting leaves.

Make sure that you don't disturb the creatures that come to live in your mammal mound. You can find out which animals these are by gently spreading some sand around the edge of the mound. The animals will leave their tracks in the sand. You'll then be able to look up the tracks in an identification guide.

If there is enough space, plan a very secluded part of the garden which cannot easily be reached by the human visitors to the garden. This will provide a quiet refuge for many creatures where they won't be disturbed.

Stocking your garden

Once you have decided where you are going to make your garden and what it will look like, you'll want to start collecting the flowers and plants which are going to grow in it. There are several ways to get hold of plants and seeds cheaply, or for no money at all.

A lot of plants, including many grasses, will appear in your garden without any help from you. These are the type of plants which depend on the wind to carry their seeds. Seeds will be blown by the wind until they reach your garden, where some of them will drop onto the ground and may take root in the soil. The plants they produce are often well suited to a wild patch or meadow.

You could collect the flowers of various grasses and use reference guides to help you to identify them. How many can you find growing in one square metre of ground? You'll need to find a patch of grass which has grown quite long and which has had time to flower.

The seeds on a Dandelion head are blown by the wind to new areas.

In parks and school playing fields the grass is usually kept so short that it never comes into flower.

Perhaps you could ask your teacher whether a strip of grass could be left uncut along one side of the playing field? A strip just one metre wide would be enough, and would only need to be cut once or twice a year.

Other plants depend on birds to spread their seeds around. Birds eat the fruit of plants such as Hawthorn and Privet, and they deposit the seeds, or pips, in new places. This can provide you with another free source of seeds.

◀ **The beaks of birds like this Greenfinch are specially shaped for seed-eating.**

Growing cycles

Plants have different growing cycles. Knowing about these will help you to decide whether to grow a plant from seed or to plant out bulbs or cuttings.

Annuals, such as Marigolds and Poppies, die at the end of the growing season each year. They drop their seeds before they die, and new plants grow from them in the spring. Annuals are often fairly simple to grow from seed.

A field of Poppies ▲

Biennials, such as Teasel and Foxgloves, have a two year growing cycle. They spend the first year growing and drop their seeds at the end of the second growing season before they die. You can grow biennials from seed.

◀ **A Teasel**

16

Perennials can be grown from seed, but it is much easier to plant them as bulbs. Many perennials, such as Cowslips and Bluebells, can even be bought as growing plants. They can be expensive to buy, but this is the quickest way of establishing them in your garden.

Other perennials, like the Buddleia, loose their leaves in winter, but don't die back above the ground completely. It is best to grow these perennials as cuttings or small plants.

Perennials stop growing in the winter, but they don't die completely. Some, such as Bluebells and Snowdrops, form a bulb underground which acts as a food store for the plant. Although the plant dies above the ground, the underground bulb is ready to grow into a new plant in the spring.

Bluebells growing in a wood ▶

People who have gardens of their own are often a good source of plants and seeds. Ask around, and tell people about your garden plan. You're sure to find some people who will be happy to give you some cuttings or seeds from healthy plants.

To take a cutting from a plant, make a diagonal cut through one of the shoots just above the place where the shoot divides from the main stem. Plant the shoot in a pot. It will soon grow roots.

Ask an adult to cut through the stem for you.

Plants from Seeds

Poppy

Teasel

Iris

Marigold

Foxglove

Plants from Bulbs

snowdrop

Bluebell

Daffodil

Hyacinth

Tulip

Seeds can be expensive to buy from shops and garden centres, although many places will give you a discount if they know it's for a school garden. It's usually easier and cheaper to buy seeds through the post. The seeds are sent with instructions about growing and planting. There is a list of addresses to write to on page 32.

You can buy mature wild plants from a wildflower nursery. This is a good way of getting your garden going quickly. Look in the telephone directory to find out the nearest wildflower nursery to your home or school.

Have a good look at the wildflowers that grow locally. These are the flowers that will probably grow best in your garden.

You could try collecting your own seeds. Find a dead flower (the flowers were still growing when this picture was taken), slip a plastic bag over its head and fasten it – not too tightly – with a rubber band. Shake the flower head gently so that the seeds fall into the bag. Flowers that drop a lot of seeds include Foxgloves, Great Mullein, Poppy, Dandelion and Iris.

Never dig up plants from the wild. It is against the law.

Planting out

Grow garden plants from seed

You will need:

peat

yoghurt pots
or peat pots

a sunny window sill

seeds

water

Fill the yoghurt pots or peat pots with peat and sprinkle a
few seeds on top. Push the seeds very gently into the peat
until they are lightly covered just under the surface. Put
the pots on a sunny windowsill and keep the peat damp.

When the seeds have grown into seedlings, they are ready to be planted out. Use a trowel to dig a hole in the earth where you want the plant to grow. If you have grown your seedling in a yoghurt pot, hold your fingers over the top of the pot and tap the bottom of it gently so that the peat comes away from the sides of the pot. You'll see the root structure that the plant has formed through the peat.

Put the seedling into the hole you've made for it and press it in gently. If you've used a peat pot, you can plant the whole pot into the ground without removing the seedling first.

Wildflowers are more difficult than garden plants to grow from seed. Many wildflower seeds need to lie on the ground throughout a whole frosty winter before they can germinate or begin to grow. It's best to sow these in early autumn for germination the following year.

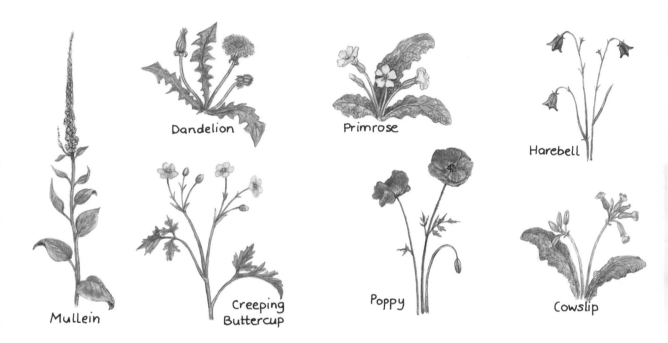

Mullein

Dandelion

Creeping Buttercup

Primrose

Poppy

Harebell

Cowslip

Primroses ▼

If you want to speed up this process, you can soak the seeds of flowers such as Primroses and Cowslips in water and leave them in the fridge for a week or two. This will create an artificial winter and it will mean that you'll be able to plant the seeds in early spring to produce flowers in the summer.

Some seed instructions suggest that you can start to grow a wildflower meadow by spreading seeds directly onto a grass-covered area without removing the grass first. This doesn't often work very well. You'll get better results if you remove the top layer of turf before sowing your wildflower seeds.

After you have removed all the turf from your meadow area, you'll need to turn the soil over, or rotovate it. This is very hard work, so make sure that there are people to help you! Sow your wildflower seeds into the rotovated soil. You could use the leftover turf and soil to form the base for a hedge or to make a flower bank or rockery in your garden area.

An easier way of making a meadow is to lift out small patches of turf in a grassy area. You can then dig over the soil underneath the turf and sow the seeds into that. This type of meadow will develop patches of wildflowers which will eventually spread.

Looking after your garden

Formal, planned gardens need different treatment to wilder, meadow areas. For example, you can use fertilizer on the plants in a formal garden to help them to grow well, but it's not a good idea to use fertilizer on your meadow.

Wildflowers have adapted to be able to grow on very poor soils where many other plants cannot survive. If the soil is improved, other kinds of plants will take over and the wildflowers may die.

Once your meadow has begun to grow, you'll need to decide how often you are going to cut it. A meadow which is cut every September will develop a different mix of plants and animals to a meadow which is cut in spring, or one which is cut twice a year.

▲ **A meadow mixture of Dandelions and Harebells.**

All cutting tools can be dangerous and some must only be used by adults. Take an adult with you whenever you want to cut your meadow area.

You could divide your meadow in half and cut each half at different times of the year. If the meadow is to develop successfully, it's important to stick to whichever timetable you decide on. You could use the grass cuttings to build compost heaps or mammal mounds.

Which tools will you use to cut your meadow? Electric machines called strimmers will cut your meadow quickly, but they need to be used very carefully as they can damage shrubs and hedges. Scythes cut the meadow without disturbing the roots of the plants. Shears are well suited for cutting small areas.

If you make a more formal flower garden, it will need to be weeded every two weeks from April until October. There are other jobs to do too, such as keeping the bird bath filled with clean water, collecting the seeds which flowers produce and watering the garden.

Plan a maintenance program for your garden and ask your family and friends to help you to keep the garden looking good.

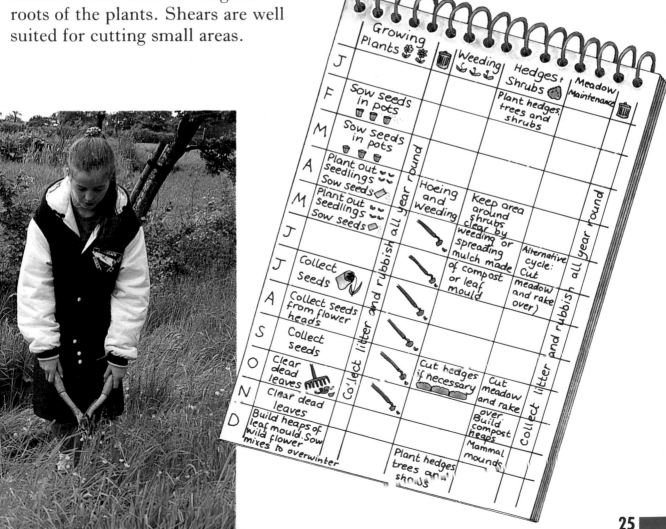

	Growing Plants 🌸🌼	🗑	Weeding 🌱🌱🌱	Hedges + Shrubs 🪨	Meadow Maintenance 🗑
J					
F	Sow seeds in pots 🪴			Plant hedges, trees and shrubs	
M	Sow seeds in pots 🪴				
A	Plant out seedlings 🌿🌿 Sow seeds 🌾	all year round	Hoeing and Weeding	Keep area around shrubs clear by weeding or spreading mulch made of compost or leaf mould	all year round
M	Plant out seedlings 🌿🌿 Sow seeds 🌾				
J				Alternative cycle: Cut meadow and rake over)	
J	Collect seeds				
A	Collect seeds from flower heads	Collect litter and rubbish			Collect litter and rubbish
S	Collect seeds				
O	Clear dead leaves		Cut hedges if necessary	Cut meadow and rake over.	
N	Clear dead leaves			Build compost heaps Mammal mounds	
D	Build heaps of leaf mould. Sow wild flower mixes to overwinter		Plant hedges trees and shrubs		

25

Investigating your garden

A few simple pieces of equipment will help you to investigate the plants and animals in your garden.

Garden investigation kit

Crayons and pencils – for sketching plants and animals. Before you sketch a flower, try to match the shade of a coloured pencil or crayon to the colour of the flower. How close a match can you get? Can you discover which colour plants are visited most often by bees? What is a butterfly's favourite colour?

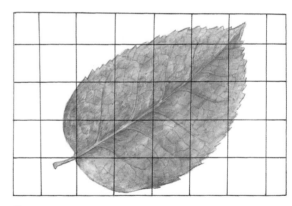

Camera – a fun way to record plants and animals.

Centimetre grid and squared paper – these are useful for helping you to draw a flower or leaf accurately to scale. Lie a 1 cm grid over the flower or leaf and carefully make a copy onto 1 cm squared paper.

Flower press – a way of recording flowers by mounting them on paper. You can make your own flower press, by putting flowers between two sheets of blotting paper and carefully piling a few heavy books on top. Leave the press for three or four days.

Mount the pressed flowers onto paper or a plant record sheet with the information you've found out about the flower.

Name of plant   Height

Date of first flower   Number of flowers

Picture of flower (scale drawing, photo or pressing)

Picture of leaf (scale drawing, photo or pressing)

Picture of seeds or fruit

Method of seed dispersal (by wind, birds etc)

Which insects visit the plant?

What happens to the plant after seeding?

Is the plant an annual, a biennial or a perennial?

Reference guides – to help you to identify the plants and animals in your garden. There is a list of reference guides on page 32. Make your own reference material by filling in a record sheet for each plant in your garden or meadow.

Hand lens – these are useful for magnifying leaves, flowers and minibeasts to study them close-up.

Quadrat – a wooden or plastic square useful for marking out an area of ground when you want to investigate the plants which are growing in a fixed area of land. You could make your own quadrat out of four strips of card. How many different types of plant are there in one square metre of your garden or meadow?

Pooter – this is useful for picking up insects without harming them.

You will need:

a rubber band

plasticine

clean polythene tubing

scissors

a plastic or glass screw-topped jar

a gimlet

a small piece of muslin or nylon stocking

Using a gimlet, make two holes in the lid of the jar which are just big enough for the tubing to pass through. Cut two pieces of tubing, one 20 cm long and the other 10 cm long. Push them into the holes in the lid of the jar and seal the gap with plasticine.

Wrap the muslin or nylon around the end of the shorter tube inside the lid. Secure it with a rubber band. The muslin or nylon acts as a filter to stop insects from being sucked into your mouth. Screw the lid back onto the jar to complete your pooter.

Practise pointing the longer tube at insects and sucking on the shorter tube. The insect will shoot up the tube into the jar without being damaged. Let the insect go as soon as you have finished studying it. Don't keep it in the pooter jar for more than a day.

Make a study of the insects which visit the plants in your garden. Some insects help to pollinate plants and collect nectar from the plants in return. Other insects eat plants, or use them to build nests in or lay eggs on them. Which of the plants in your garden or meadow benefit from their contact with insects and which are harmed by insects?

Gardens and meadows never stop changing. During the winter, you'll see few signs of life apart from evergreen plants which do not lose their leaves in cold weather. The first flowers begin to appear in the spring. Before long, all sorts of plants will be competing for every available patch of soil.

Follow the growing cycles of the plants in your garden or meadow throughout the year. Watch the first shoots appear and follow the growing cycle through flowering, pollination and seed dispersal.

Use photographs, pictures and record sheets to build up an information bank of the changes which take place during each season. You could make an illustrated diary of a whole year's activity in your garden or meadow.

Every year, more of our countryside is threatened. Building work, farming, pollution and many other human activities are destroying meadows, hedgerows, marshes and ponds. As these wildflower habitats disappear, many plants are becoming increasingly rare.

By making gardens and meadows at home or at school, you will be providing an important refuge for wildflowers and the creatures who depend on them for food and shelter.

Index

Useful addresses

British Trust for Conservation Volunteers
10–14 Duke Street, Reading, Berks. RG1 4RU.
Watch
22, The Green, Nettleham, Lincoln LN22 2RR.
(Watch runs a conservation club for children.)
English Nature, Northminster House,
Northminster, Peterborough PE1 1UA.

Seed Suppliers

Emorsgate Seeds
Middle Cottage, Emorsgate, Terrington St
Clement, Kings Lynn, Norfolk.
School Garden Company
P.O. Box 49, Spalding, Lincs. PE11 1NZ.
John Chambers Wildflower Seeds
15 Westleigh Road, Barton Seagrave, Kettering,
Northants NN15 5AJ.

Reference guides

Flowers (Clue Book)
G. Allen and J. Denslow (OUP).
Trees (Clue Book)
G. Allen and J. Denslow (OUP).
Flowerless Plants
G. Allen and J. Denslow (OUP).
Collins Pocket Guide to Wild Flowers
McClintock & Fitter (Collins).
The Usborne Nature Trail Book of Garden Wildlife
Su Swallow (Usborne).
Food for Free
Richard Mabey (Arrow Books).
Back to the Roots
Richard Mabey (Arrow Books).
A Dyer's Manual
Jill Goodwin (Pelham Books).